What People Are Sayin

Prayer Themes and Guided Meditations for Children

"Barbara Ann Bretherton has provided teachers and parents with an excellent tool to help children pray using their imaginations and their bodies. *Prayer Themes and Guided Meditations for Children* offers a practical, step-by-step approach to nurturing a child's personal relationship with God. It deserves a place in every classroom and home."

Kathleen Finley
Author, *Dear God: Prayers for Families with Children*
and *Our Family Book of Days*

"I'm going to tell everyone I know who teaches religion or who prays with children to get this book. Each meditation is beautifully constructed and written so that it can be used with people of all ages. I appreciate the variety of prayer themes that are truly in touch with children's daily lives. I also value the solid links of these meditations to traditional prayers and to Scripture. Any catechists new to leading children in meditation will be put at ease by the clear instructions and everyday language in this book. Veteran catechists will welcome Barabara Ann Bretherton's creativity and fresh approaches to prayer with students."

Peg Bowman
Author, *At Home With the Sacraments:*
Baptism, Eucharist, Confirmation, and Reconciliation

"*Prayer Themes and Guided Meditations for Children* allows children of all ages to experience prayer in a magical and wonderful way. The themes addressed are very relevant to the experiences of children as they experience God in their lives throughout the year. This is a wonderful resource for both parents and children alike.

"Ms. Bretherton has organized the presentation of the material in a very easy-to-follow manner. I especially like the preparation activities which bring the prayer experience to life, making it more concrete for the child. I look forward to using this resource with the children with whom I work. It is truly a gift to our prayer experiences."

Gayle Schreiber
Author, *Prayer Services for Young Children* and *Saints Alive*

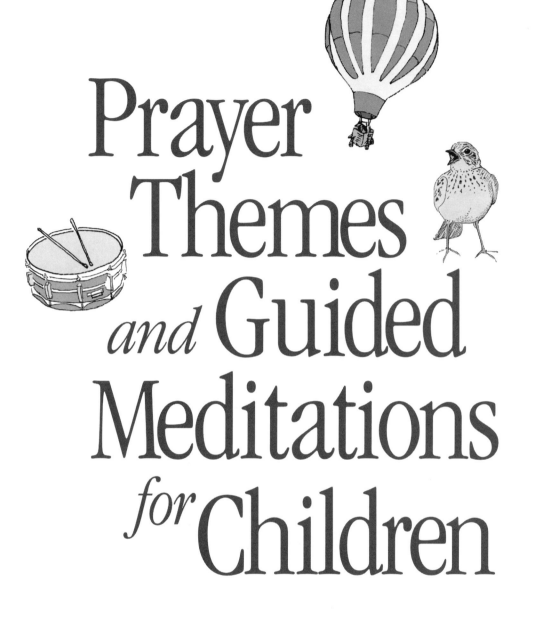

Prayer Themes *and* Guided Meditations *for* Children

Barbara Ann Bretherton

XXIII

TWENTY-THIRD PUBLICATIONS

Mystic, CT 06355

North American Edition 1998

Originally published in 1997 as *You and Me God: Prayer Themes and Guided Meditations for Children* by Social Science Press, Wentworth Falls, NSW, Australia.

Twenty-Third Publications
185 Willow Street
P.O. Box 180
Mystic, CT 06355
(860) 536-2611
(800) 321-0411

ISBN 0-89622-896-7
Library of Congress Catalog Card Number 97-62343
Printed in the U.S.A.

Acknowledgments

This work could not have been completed without the tireless effort of my friend and colleague Barbara Fyfe. Her suggestions regarding the readability of the text and her advice and assistance with the layout of the book are much appreciated.

Most of all I wish to thank Barbara for her constant support and encouragement during the writing of the meditations and for her willingness to share in the overall task of producing a work aimed at assisting teachers and parents to bring children closer to God in prayer.

Contents

Prayer Themes *and* Guided Meditations *for* Children

Introduction

Meditation and contemplation have a long and treasured place in the Christian prayer tradition.

Throughout the centuries many people have recognized the benefits of pondering on the mysteries of faith and of withdrawing from the clamor of busy lives to spend time in quiet solitude and friendship with God.

The Catechism of the Catholic Church tells us that meditative prayer uses thought, imagination, emotion, and desire to deepen faith, bring about a change of heart, and strengthen the will to follow Jesus and his way of life (CCC 2708).

When speaking of contemplative prayer, the Catechism quotes St. Teresa of Avila who says: "Contemplative prayer...is nothing else than a close sharing between friends; it means taking time frequently to be alone with him who we know loves us..." Jesus, and in him, the Father (CCC 2709).

Meditation and contemplation enable the Christian to encounter God in a deeply personal and intimate manner.

Children and students of all ages can be introduced to and experience meditative and contemplative prayer. These simple yet profound forms of imaginative prayer make real for them the presence of God in their lives—a God who loves them and accompanies them at each step along life's journey.

Imaginative prayer 1) provides an opportunity for children to hear the Word of God speaking to them through the Scriptures, 2) gives children time and space to enter into personal conversation and friendship with God, and 3) assists children in discovering the presence of God within them thus enabling them to meet God deep within their hearts. The challenge for the teacher, catechist, and parent is to show the children how!

Prayer Themes and Guided Meditations for Children assists teachers, catechists, and parents to guide children in the way of meditative and contemplative prayer—prayer of the mind and heart.

How to Use this Book

Prayer Themes and Guided Meditations for Children draws upon the everyday faith and life experiences of children and uses these as a source for prayer.

The book is a how-to, easy to read and follow religious education resource which enables teachers, parents, and catechists to lead children into imaginative prayer. The prayer themes chosen incorporate concepts and ideas common to the lives and interests of children. A number of the meditations also reflect significant events in the Christian calendar.

The meditations vary in length and style. They provide the teacher or parent with a variety of approaches for different levels of ability and maturity. The language, concepts, and ideas are adaptable and may be simplified or extended as desired.

Each meditation is preceded by a number of suggested teaching/learning activities and strategies ("Preparation") which provide a context for the prayer experience. It is strongly recommended that these activities, or similar ones chosen by the teacher or parent, be seen as integral to the meditation experience.

The Process

It is important that each meditation is read slowly and calmly. The right pace is more likely to be achieved if the prayer leader prays along with the children.

A quiet, comfortable environment will aid concentration. Dimmed lighting and soft instrumental music may contribute to the creation of a prayerful atmosphere.

Each guided meditation comprises four basic steps:

RELAX   FOCUS   PONDER   PRAY

Relax. During this phase of the meditation the children are prepared for prayer through a suggested relaxation activity. This activity is designed to help them enter the prayer time relaxed but alert. The activities have been chosen to complement a particular prayer theme. Prayer leaders may wish to simplify or adapt these activities to suit the age of the child.

Focus. In this section of the meditation, the children are encouraged through observation and exploration to focus on an object or group of objects before them. (Such objects will have been created or collected during preparation for the prayer session).

The intention during this phase is to gain the children's total attention and have them concentrate on the central idea or theme of the prayer.

Ponder. Here the children are led into reflection upon the theme or object of the prayer. This meditative part of the prayer process provides the basis for the children's personal conversation with God.

Pray. This is the moment of intimate and personal encounter with God through prayer. The children are invited in their imagination to enter into their heart or "special meeting place" where they feel comfortable and can be alone in conversation with God—Father, Son, and Holy Spirit. It is important that this phase of the meditation be approached with sensitivity so that the children have sufficient time and space to share with God their personal thoughts and feelings.

Conclusion. The meditation is brought to a close through a re-entry phase where the children are gently led back to the classroom or home situation.

Follow-up activities help to round off the prayer time and consolidate the learning.

> *Guide children in prayer and you have*
> *given them a most precious gift for life.*

Family

Preparation

•Have the children draw/bring a picture of members of their families.

•Gather the children around a prayer mat/table on which is placed a picture or image of Jesus' family—Jesus, Mary, and Joseph—a lighted candle, and a Bible.

•Include on the prayer mat/table, photos or pictures of children's own families and a picture of a hot air balloon.

Meditation

Read the following guided meditation to the children.

Relaxation Exercise

Today we are going to talk with God about our families.

Sit straight and tall and imagine you are about to take a ride in a hot air balloon.

First we need to fill the balloon with air, so that it can float up into the sky.

Breathe deeply and freely.

Breathe in and out...in and out.

Picture the balloon filling up with clean, fresh air.

Now close your eyes and imagine yourself in the balloon floating up into the sky.

See yourself climbing higher and higher.

Focus

Look down at the earth from the balloon.

See the football field...the trees in the park...

the roads and the cars taking people to work.

Look down again and see the school.

Suddenly you see your own house.

What does it look like from so high up in the sky?

Imagine that your family is out in the backyard.

They are looking up at you and waving to you.

Who can you see?

Feel how excited they are to see you floating overhead.

In your mind wave back to them.

Let your family see what fun you are having.

Ponder

Think for a moment how good it is to have a family who cares for you and is interested in everything that you do.

Families are special to each one of us.

They are God's precious gift to us.

It is important to remember them and to show them that we love them.

Pray

Keep your eyes closed.

Now imagine that Jesus is with you in the balloon.

He too can see your family.

Tell him about them—their names and something special about each one.

Jesus loves to hear you talk about your family.

Remember that Jesus has a family too.

Listen to Jesus tell you about Mary, his mother,

and Joseph, his foster father who was a carpenter.

Mary and Joseph taught Jesus many things when he was a child.

As you listen, you can tell that Jesus loves his family...

and that he loves your family too.

Jesus tells you how special your family is...

how God has given them to you to love you...

and to help you grow into a good person.

Tell Jesus that you are glad you have a family who loves you and cares for you.

Ask Jesus to send them a special blessing.

Watch him as he raises his hands in blessing over your house and your family.

Conclusion

Your balloon is now moving away from your house and coming in to land near the school.

Watch the air slowly leave the balloon as it brings you back down to earth.

You are now safely back on the ground.

Picture yourself walking away from the balloon and returning to the classroom.

Concentrate again on your own breathing.

Breathe in and out...in and out...in and out.

When you are ready, open your eyes and look at the picture of your family.

Pick it up and hold it.

Be happy that Jesus has blessed your family today.

Say thank you to God for each member of your family.

Invite the children to write a prayer thanking God for their families. They might also make a thank-you card for their families.

Jesus' Mother Is My Mother

Preparation

•Prepare a prayer mat/table on which is placed a picture or statue of Mary holding the child Jesus.

•Include on the mat/table a candle, flowers, and a children's Bible opened at a picture of Mary.

•Gather the children around the prayer mat/table.

Meditation

Read the following guided meditation to the children.

Relaxation Exercise

Today we are going to think about Mary, the mother of Jesus.

Mary is also our mother.

She takes care of us just as she cared for Jesus.

Close your eyes.

Listen carefully to your breathing and the quiet beating of your heart.

Breathe deeply and slowly.

Feel the air entering your body, giving it life and energy.

Breathe in and out...in and out...in and out.

Feel comfortable and relaxed.

Focus

Open your eyes and look at the image of Mary on the prayer mat/table.

Notice how Mary holds Jesus close to her in her arms.

Mary and Jesus are always close to each other because Mary is Jesus' mother and they love each other very much.

Mary looked after Jesus when he was a baby.

When he was growing up she taught him all about the customs of his people and how to be a good Jewish boy.

Mary was a wonderful mother to Jesus,

and she stayed close to him always...

even when he was being crucified on the cross by the soldiers.

Mary is our mother too.

She will help us in the same way that she helped and cared for Jesus.

Ponder

Close your eyes and picture yourself with your own mother, or the person who is like a mother to you and cares for you.

Think of all the things a mother does for you...

preparing your food...washing your clothes...taking you places...

cleaning the house...looking after you when you are sick...

spending time with you...helping you with things you want to do...

encouraging you with your school-work...your sports...your dancing...your music.

Think of the things your mother or caregiver teaches you...

how to be happy and good...how to say please and thank you...

how to show respect for others...how to be kind and helpful...

how to be strong and stand tall, especially when you feel sad or are hurting.

Remember how your mother hugs you and holds you close when you need to be comforted.

God gave us our mothers/caregivers.

They are very special people in our lives.

Mary is also our mother.

She also takes care of us...teaches us...and helps us to grow up like Jesus.

Pray

Keeping your eyes closed, use your imagination to take you into your heart or special place where you can be alone and where you usually talk with Jesus.

As you enter your special place today, imagine that Mary is there.

See Mary waiting for you...encouraging you to come close to her.

Feel the softness of her long dress and cloak as she takes your hand and holds you close.

Let her draw you near to her.

Feel the love she has for you.

Imagine that you sit down beside Mary...or on her lap.

Hear her ask you how you are feeling...

and if you would like to tell her anything.

Talk to Mary for a few moments just as you talk to your mother or caregiver.

Mary likes to listen to your stories and your requests.

Pause

Now listen as Mary tells you how much she loves you and that she is always there for you…

that you can talk to her anytime and she will always listen.

Say thank you to Mary and tell her it is time for you to go.

Say good-bye to Mary.

Leave your special place and slowly return to the classroom.

As you leave, remember that Mary is always there for you.

She is your heavenly mother, who cares for you like she cared for Jesus.

Conclusion

As you return to the classroom, focus again on your breathing.

Breathe deeply and slowly…in and out…in and out…in and out.

When you are ready, open you eyes and look at the picture/statue on the table/mat.

Remember that Mary is Jesus' mother and your mother too.

Invite children to say or sing the Hail Mary.

I Believe in Angels

This meditation is best prayed around the time of the feast of the Holy Guardian Angels (October 2).

Preparation

•Discuss with the children the place of angels in the Jewish and Christian traditions. Focus on angels as:

—servants and messengers of God…

—intelligent beings who are like God's agents…

—acting for God in our world…

—announcing God's plan for us…

—carefully watching over us…

—helping us…praying with us and for us.

(Catechism of the Catholic Church 328, 329, 336)

•Share with the children Scripture stories which tell of the presence and work of angels as messengers of God. God sent his angels to:

—Tell Abraham not to sacrifice his son, Isaac *(Genesis 22:11–13);*

—Save Hagar and her son *(Genesis 21:15–20);*

—Accompany Tobit on his journey to Media *(Tobit 5);*

—Tell Mary she would become the mother of Jesus *(Luke 1:26–38);*

—Announce the birth of Jesus and sing God's praises *(Luke 2:8–14);*

—Strengthen Jesus in his agony *(Luke 22:41–43);*

—Witness to Jesus' resurrection *(Mark 16:1–7);*

—Care for the apostles and save them from prison so they could continue to preach God's Word *(Acts 5:17–21).*

•Have the children write one of these stories in their own words.

•Allow the children to discuss appropriate videos/movies or stories that involve angels. Link them to the Judaeo-Christian belief in angels so that the children's understandings are based on sound teaching.

•Prepare a prayer table/mat on which is placed a Bible opened at one of the references to angels, a picture of an angel, a lighted candle, and some of the children's written stories about angels.

•Gather the children around the prayer table/mat.

Meditation

Read the following guided meditation to the children.

Relaxation Exercise

Today we are going to talk with Jesus about angels…

creatures created by God to watch over each one of us,

and to help us know God and God's love for us.

First we need to relax.

As you know, angels are spirits, therefore they are weightless.

Close your eyes and imagine for a few moments that you too are weightless.

Breathe deeply and slowly.

See yourself floating in the air like a feather or a large leaf.

Breathe in and out…in and out…in and out.

Now picture yourself gently floating back to rest peacefully on the ground.

Feel happy, relaxed, and ready to pray.

Focus

Open your eyes now.

Sit tall and straight with your legs crossed.

Place your hands loosely in your lap.

During the past few days we have been learning about God's angels.

You know that angels are intelligent beings whom God has created to be his messengers.

Angels help us on our journey of life…

they help us to know God,

to worship him and to follow his ways.

God has given each of us a guardian angel to protect us from harm and to keep us on the road to heaven.

God's angels are constant workers.

In heaven they sing God's praises.

On earth they work quietly,

helping to bring about God's kingdom…

a kingdom of justice, love, and peace.

Ponder

Now close your eyes again and recall the stories you have heard and written about God's angels.

God sends his angels to help people…

to guide them…

to direct their actions…

to protect them from harm…

to strengthen them in times of trouble and difficulty.

Think how the angels know who God is…

how they adore God in heaven…

how they sing God's praises with heavenly songs and words:

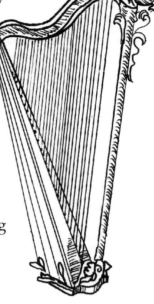

> *Holy, Holy, Holy Lord,*
>
> *God of power and might,*
>
> *Heaven and earth are filled with your glory.*
>
> *Hosanna in the highest.*

You too can join with the angels in praising God.

You do this every time you go to Mass.

Pray

Now go into your heart or special place where Jesus is always waiting for you.

As you enter your special place, imagine that Jesus is surrounded by angels.

They look just like you imagine them to be…

dressed in white robes and bearing wings.

They make a beautiful sound as they sing God's praise.

See Jesus invite you to listen to their song.

As you listen you hear them sing a prayer that you know:

> *Glory to God in the highest*
>
> *And peace on earth to people of good will.*

The presence of the angels makes you feel happy and comfortable.

Jesus enjoys their presence too.

Now, look at Jesus.

He is beckoning you to come closer so you can hear what he has to say to you.

Hear Jesus tell you that the angels are God's workers…

they help you to know God, to love God, and to choose what is right.

Jesus tells you that God's angels will protect you from evil and sin…

they will help you know what true happiness is and how good God is.

Jesus reminds you that God has appointed a guardian angel just for you…

that you have a special angel to help you on your Christian journey.

Tell Jesus how happy you are knowing you have a holy guardian angel to watch over you.

Conclusion

Now it is time for you to leave your special place.

As you turn to leave and make your way back to the classroom, you hear the angels singing in the distance.

The sound becomes softer and softer and gradually fades away.

When you are ready, open you eyes and look at the Bible and the picture on the prayer table/mat.

Remember that God has appointed angels to take care of you.

Your guardian angel is always at your side.

Teach the children the following verse:

Angel of God, my guardian dear,

To whom God's love commits me here,

Ever this day be at my side,

To light and guard,

To rule and guide.

Amen.

God Things

Preparation

•Have the children bring to the prayer session a religious gift or memento from home. This may be a holy picture, medal, rosary, bracelet, Bible, statue, prayer book, crucifix, baptism candle.

•Ensure each child knows something of the story of the memento:

—To whom does it belong?

—When was it obtained?

—Is it special for someone?

—What makes it special?

—Where is it kept at home?

•Have ready a tape of quiet instrumental music.

•Gather the children around a prayer table or mat on which is placed a large candle, a Bible, and a centerpiece of cardboard on which is written "God Things."

•Have the children place or hold in front of them their sacred symbol or object. (Make sure you have a few extra holy cards for those children who forget to bring something—a card which they can keep.)

Meditation

Read the following guided meditation to the children.

Relaxation Exercise

Today we are going to talk with God about sacred things that remind us of God's presence.

Close your eyes and breathe slowly so that you can enter the prayer time in a peaceful and calm manner.

Play some background music without words.

Listen carefully to the music.

Listen especially for the deep, low notes that are way down under the melody line.

Listen well because these notes are often hidden beneath the colorful, high notes of the orchestra.

Enjoy the music.

Feel comfortable and relaxed.

After a few moments, turn down the volume of the music. When the children are truly settled, continue.

Focus

Open your eyes.

Focus on the sacred object, or God Thing, which you have brought to the session.

Think of the story of your sacred memento.

Perhaps you would like to share something about your memento with the class.

It is important for the prayer leader to provide an example so that this part of the prayer is not too long: I have brought my favorite picture of Jesus. It was given to me by a very good friend. It hangs in our kitchen. When I look at it, I can talk to Jesus and remember that he is always with me.

Ponder

Place your object on the floor in front of you.

Close your eyes.

Picture in your imagination your special God Thing.

See it wherever it is usually kept at home.

Think about where it came from…to whom it belongs…why you have it in your home.

What does your God Thing remind you of?

Think how sacred objects are ways to remember that God is always near us…

how they can help us talk to God and share our lives with God.

Pray

Now go into your heart or special place where Jesus is always waiting to greet you.

Tell him the story of your God Thing.

Show it to him.

Perhaps you have some questions to ask him.

Pause

Offer your sacred memento to Jesus.

See him take it with gentleness and delight.

Hear Jesus say how glad he is that you have a sacred memento…

something to help you remember that God is your special friend…

and that God is always with you.

Listen as Jesus tells you he would like you to put your God Thing in a special place where you can see it often…

a place where it will remind you of your friendship with God.

See Jesus give you back your sacred memento.

See yourself take hold of it with care.

Look at Jesus and tell him where you will put your special God Thing in your house.

Tell Jesus that you will try to remember to look at it each day and say a prayer for someone.

Conclusion

Now slowly leave your heart or special place and return to the classroom.

Pick up your sacred memento, your God Thing, from the floor in front of you.

Look at it as you hold it gently.

Take a moment to say a short prayer for someone you love.

Pause

Now place your special memento on the prayer table/mat.

We will leave it there today to remind us that God is our friend and is with us always.

Favorite Hobbies

Preparation

•Invite the children to share with the class their favorite hobbies and why they enjoy these particular activities.

•Where appropriate allow some children to present their favorite hobby to the class by means of the guessing game Charades.

•Encourage the children to bring a symbol of their favorite hobby to the prayer session.

•Cover the prayer table with a brightly colored cloth and upon it place a lighted candle, a picture of Jesus, and some symbols of the children's favorite hobbies.

•Gather the children around the prayer table.

Meditation

Read the following guided meditation to the children.

Relaxation Exercise

Today we are going to share with Jesus our favorite hobbies.

First let us relax our bodies and prepare ourselves to quietly enter the prayer time.

Sit tall and straight with your legs stretched out in front of you.

Place your hands palms down on the floor beside you.

Close your eyes.

Breathe in a long deep breath…hold it for a couple of seconds…then gently let your breath out.

Do this again, but this time as you breathe in, stiffen your knees and push them down to the floor.

Hold this position for a couple of seconds…then breathe out and relax your knees and your whole body.

Repeat this exercise a couple of times…stiffening your knees…then relaxing them…stiffening…then relaxing…stiffening…then relaxing.

Now cross your legs and sit straight and tall with your hands in your lap.

Breathe in a deep breath and hold for a few seconds.

As you do, squeeze your hands and your feet tightly into a ball.

Breathe out, relax your hands and feet and your whole body.

Do this again and concentrate on tightening your muscles and then letting go…tightening and letting go…tightening and letting go.

Breathe in and out a few more times.

Tell your body to feel relaxed and at peace.

Focus

Open your eyes now and look at the symbols on and around the prayer table.

Each of these symbols tells a story of the things you and your classmates like to do.

Some like to play sports, others like to sing and dance.

Some like to make things, others like to grow plants.

Some of you are bookworms, others like to write.

Some of you enjoy riding around on your bikes.

Some of you are team players, others are supporters of those who play.

Some prefer computer games to test their skill or to pass their time away.

Some of you like to listen, others like to chat.

Some of you are only happy swinging a ball and a bat.

Some like to relax on their own, others like being with friends.

Some like to focus on real games, others just like to pretend.

Whatever you do it is special to you.

You are the one who enjoys your play…

each of you in your own special way.

Ponder

Close your eyes and take a few moments now to think about the things you really like to do in your spare time.

Choose one of these things to focus on today.

Picture yourself at the spot where your favorite hobby usually takes place.

Name the place in your mind.

Who is with you?

Family…friends…team members… or are you there by yourself?

Is your favorite hobby part of a competition or is it just for fun?

What do you like best about the hobby?

How often do you get the chance to participate in this activity?

How does it make you feel?

Do other people enjoy this activity too?

Who likes to share in your favorite hobby?

Some of the most wonderful moments in your life come from doing things you enjoy and having fun with family or friends.

These are moments you will remember long after they are over.

When you are older, you will tell stories about the things you enjoy doing now.

Enjoying life brings happiness to you and to those who love and care for you.

God also likes to see you laughing and enjoying yourself.

Pray

Now go into your heart or special place where you can share your good times with Jesus.

He is waiting for you, happy to see you, and looking forward to talking with you.

Imagine you hear Jesus say hello to you, welcome you, and invite you to sit down beside him.

Listen as Jesus asks you to share your story with him.

Tell Jesus about your favorite hobby.

Tell him why you like your chosen hobby.

Share with him something about the pleasure this activity gives you.

Jesus loves to hear your stories and to see you happy.

Take a few moments to talk with Jesus.

Pause

When you have finished your story, look at Jesus and see how happy he is.

Hear him tell you how much he loves to see you enjoying the life that God has given to you…

how it makes him happy to see you learning new skills and feeling good about yourself.

Listen as Jesus thanks you for sharing your favorite hobby with him.

Hear him tell you that God has given you many gifts and God is delighted to see you using them.

Say yes to Jesus.

Now it is time to leave Jesus in your heart or special place and return to the classroom.

See yourself stand up together with Jesus, shake hands, and promise to meet with him again to share stories and spend some time together.

Conclusion

Imagine yourself leaving Jesus and making your way back to the classroom.

You are feeling good about yourself.

Now become conscious of your breathing.

Breathe in and out…in and out…in and out.

Feel happy, contented, and relaxed.

When you are ready, open your eyes.

Look again at the symbol of your favorite activity.

Remember your conversation with Jesus.

As you look forward to the next time you will participate in your favorite activity, know that Jesus enjoys your favorite activity too. Say yes to yourself.

Invite children to write about or illustrate their favorite hobby. On the back of the drawing they could compose a prayer thanking God for life and happy times.

Gifted for Others

Preparation

•Encourage the children to identify gifted and talented people in their neighborhood or parish and to write about how these people use their gifts and talents to help others.

•Have the children discuss their own gifts and talents and state how these gifts can be used to help others or make others happy.

•Tell the children the story of the talents from the gospel of Matthew *(Matthew 25:14–30)*.

•Prepare a prayer mat/table on which is placed a lighted candle, a Bible open at the story of the talents, and a vase of flowers of different varieties and colors.

•Around the prayer mat/table arrange some decorated cards on which are written gifts and talents of the children in the class, for example:

happy smile	*creative ideas*
math wizard	*helpful personality*
beautiful voice	*deep thinker*
good at sports	*friendly*
artistic	*good listener*
loyal	*generous*
fun to be with	*caring*

Make sure there are enough cards for each child to claim one as his/her own.

•Gather the children in a circle around the prayer mat/table.

Meditation

Read the following guided meditation to the children.

Relaxation Exercise

Today in our prayer time we are going to talk with Jesus about the gifts and talents God has given to us and how we can use them to benefit others.

Sit tall and upright like the flowers in the vase on the prayer mat/table.

Straighten your back and place your hands loosely in your lap.

Breathe slowly and deliberately…in and out…in and out…in and out.

Let your body feel alert but relaxed.

Focus

Look at the vase of flowers on the table.

Notice how there are many different kinds of flowers and many different colors.

The different kinds of flowers and their different colors make the vase look very pretty and attractive.

Some flowers are soft and bending…others are strong and tall.

Some are large and easily seen…others are small and you need to look hard to notice them.

Look at the greenery that surrounds the flowers.

Notice that there are many different shades of green.

All of these together help to make the vase of flowers beautiful and enjoyable to look at.

Now look at the cards around the prayer mat.

On these cards are written some of the many gifts and talents you have been given by God.

Just like the flowers in the vase there are many different gifts and talents in our class.

Invite the children to quietly stand and choose a card from the prayer mat/table—a card that names one of their special gifts. Then, have them return to the prayer circle and place their card on the floor in front of them.

Ponder

Look at your card and think about the gift you have chosen.

Think how you enjoy this gift, and how using it makes you feel happy.

Take a moment to remember a recent time when you enjoyed using this gift which has been given to you by God.

Now remember the story of the eight talents which Jesus told to his followers.

In this story you learned how God wants you to use your gifts not only for yourself but also to help others and to make other people happy.

Think of a time when you have used your gift to make others happy or to help them in some way.

You may wish to write about this after our prayer time.

Pray

Close your eyes now and use your imagination to take you into your heart or special place where you can talk with Jesus.

See him welcome you and smile at you as you enter your special place.

Jesus loves to share these conversations with you.

Imagine that you have taken your card with you—the card that names one of the special gifts you have been given.

See Jesus ask you to show him your card.

Watch him as he smiles with delight when he reads the gift written on your card.

Jesus knows how happy this gift makes you.

He too is happy that you have this gift.

Listen to Jesus as he tells you how precious this gift is...how it makes you special and how you can use it to help others and make them happy.

Share with Jesus a time when you enjoyed using your gift and others enjoyed it too.

Hear Jesus tell you that God is pleased when you use the gift you have been given.

Tell him you will try to develop your gift further so that it will always be a special part of you.

See Jesus smile with joy at your intention.

Conclusion

Now prepare to leave your heart or special place.

Imagine yourself bringing your card back with you into the classroom.

Breathe slowly and deliberately as you return.

Breathe in and out…in and out…in and out.

When you are ready open your eyes and look at the gift card on the floor in front of you.

Remember your conversation with Jesus.

Now look again at the vase of flowers on the prayer mat/table.

Whenever you see a beautiful vase of flowers like this, remember the many different gifts that people have to enjoy and to offer to others.

Say thank you to God for the wonderful gifts and talents God has given to each of us.

Encourage the children to write about their gifts and talents and illustrate how they can use them to help others.

What's in a Name?

Preparation

•Have the children research and write about the origins and meanings of their given names.

•Encourage the children to share their stories with each other.

•Explain to the children how they are called by this name when they are baptized. It is the name by which they are welcomed into the family of the church. God knows and calls them by their names.

•Discuss the genealogy of Jesus *(Matthew 1:1–17)*. This list of ancestors places Jesus in the line of Abraham and of David from whom was to be born the messiah.

•Discuss the importance of biblical names to both Hebrew and Christian communities:

—Hebrew names often signified a certain role, power, or characteristic of the person so named.

—They called God Yahweh, which means I am who am. This was the name revealed by God to Moses. It was considered very sacred by the Jews and carried with it the power of God *(Exodus 3:14)*.

—When the angel Gabriel appeared to Mary and Joseph, he told them the son who was to be born of Mary—the Son of God— was to be called Jesus, which means savior or one who saves *(Luke 1:31–34 & Matthew 1:21)*.

—When Jesus called Simon son of John to follow him and become the leader of the Apostles, he gave him the name Peter which means rock *(John 1:42)*.

•Prepare cards or a tablecloth containing the children's given names.

• Gather the children around a prayer mat/table which is decorated with the special name cloth or name cards, a picture of Jesus, the Bible opened at the genealogy of Jesus *(Matthew 1:1–17)*, a lighted candle, and some flowers.

Meditation

Read the following guided meditation to the children.

Relaxation Exercise

Today we are going to talk with Jesus about our names.

We can use the rhythm of our names to help us relax and prepare for our prayer.

Sit tall and straight with your hands resting loosely in your lap.

Close your eyes and begin to breathe slowly and deeply.

In…out…in…out…in…out.

Now, as you breathe in, say your name in your mind and, as you breathe out, say to yourself the word relax.

Breathe in	*Breathe out*
Benjamin	*Relax*
Rosemary	*Relax*
Matthew	*Relax*
Lisa	*Relax*

Do this a few times.

Concentrate on relaxing your body as you say the name given to you by your parents.

Breathe in and out…in and out…in and out.

Let your whole body feel loose and relaxed, comfortable but alert.

Focus

Now open your eyes.

Look at your name on the tablecloth or card.

Remember the story of your name…why your parents chose it for you.

Recall how it is the name by which you were welcomed into God's family, the church.

This name is not only the name by which everyone here knows you, it is also the name by which God knows you and loves you.

God says to you: I have called you by your name; you are mine *(Isaiah 43:1).*

Ponder

Now close your eyes again and together we will think about how special it is to be called by our names.

Your name identifies you and introduces you to new people and new friends.

When someone uses your name it means they know you…they know who you are and can begin to form a friendship with you.

Your name is special because it is yours.

Even if someone else has the same name as you, your name is important and special for you.

Your name also identifies you as a member of God's family.

When you were baptized, you were welcomed into the family of God.

Your name then became your Christian name.

The word Christian means follower of Jesus.

Jesus knows you by name.

At your baptism Jesus became your brother and friend.

Jesus welcomed you into his family.

Names have meanings.

You have already discovered the meaning of your name.

Take a moment to think about this meaning.

Is there a special quality or characteristic associated with your name?

Does your name encourage you to be a special kind of person?

Perhaps your name is associated with a member of your extended family…passed down to you from one generation to the next.

What does it mean to carry this particular family name?

What special memory, quality, or characteristic does this name have in your family?

If your name has no historical meaning, what meaning would you like it to have?

Names can help us to develop important qualities.

How does having your name help you to be a better person…a better Christian?

Pray

Keep your eyes closed and go into your heart or special place where Jesus and you can be alone and talk together.

As you enter your special place, hear Jesus call you by your name and welcome you.

Jesus knows you have been learning about your name.

Imagine that you and Jesus sit down together.

Jesus asks you to tell him what is special about your name...what you like about it.

Take a few moments to share the story of your name with Jesus.

Pause

Now listen as Jesus tells you that his name is special too...that God has given him power through his name to help you, to heal you, and to save you from sin.

Jesus' name means savior.

Hear Jesus tell you that when you call on his name with reverence and faith, he can help you.

Jesus likes you to pray to him and talk with him about all the people and all the things that are part of your life.

Tell Jesus you are glad he knows you by name and that he hears you when you talk to him.

Tell him you will talk to him often.

As you stand up to leave, see Jesus offer to bless you.

Imagine that Jesus comes to you...puts his hands on your head...calls you by your name...and says: May you be blessed with peace, friendship, and love.

Be happy that you are blessed by Jesus, who is not only your brother and friend, but Jesus, Son of God.

Conclusion

Now it is time to leave your heart or special place and return to the classroom.

As you turn to leave Jesus, hear him once again say your name as he bids you good-bye for now.

When you are ready open your eyes and look again at the name on the card or tablecloth...

the name that is special to you…

the name you have been given by your parents.

Remember that Jesus knows and loves you by this name too.

Invite the children to suspend their name cards as mobiles or to leave the cards on the prayer table along with the name of Jesus as a reminder of the prayer time and the importance to God of each child's name.

A Very Special Birthday

A Christmas meditation

Preparation

• Have the children investigate the story of their own birth and early days of life. Focus on such details as:

—where they were born;

—who was present at the birth;

—who came to visit; and

—any specifically happy, traumatic, or anxious moments surrounding the event which are still remembered today by parents or family members.

• Prior to the prayer time, share some of these stories.

• Gather the children around a prayer mat/table on which is placed a Christmas crib or a picture of the birth of Jesus, a candle, and some baby photos of the children.

• Light the candle. While doing so, remind the children that the lighted candle is a sign of the presence of Jesus who is with us when we pray.

Meditation

Read the following guided meditation to the children.

Relaxation Exercise

Today in our prayer time we are going to talk with Jesus about birthdays—yours and his.

First we need to clear our minds and relax our bodies.

Sit straight and tall.

Close your eyes and imagine you are looking at a large birthday cake decorated with lighted candles.

Watch the candles flickering before you and breathe deeply and slowly as you prepare to blow them out with…one…long…breath.

Breathe in and out…in and out…in and out.

Now take a long deep breath and see yourself blowing out all the candles on the cake.

Breathe deeply and slowly a few more times and feel pleased with your effort.

Birthday cakes are a reminder of the day we were born.

They help us to celebrate each new year of life with joy and thanksgiving.

Focus

Open your eyes now and look at the prayer table/mat.

See the baby photos and the crib.

Take a moment to remember the story of your own birth…

where it took place…

who was there…

who came to visit…

who brought you gifts and presents.

Recall any special story your parents have told you about your birth…

happy…anxious…or funny moments they may have shared with you.

Pause

Look at the crib.

It tells the story of Jesus' birth which took place in the town of Bethlehem.

Jesus was not born in a hospital but most likely in a cave in the hillside around Bethlehem or in a stable or barn attached to a house.

Jesus' parents were there…Mary his mother…and Joseph his foster father.

The shepherds from the country-side came to visit…and the wise men brought Jesus gifts.

Ponder

Close your eyes now and listen to the story of Jesus' birth.

It happened on a cold night in the town of Bethlehem in the countryside of Judea.

Mary and Joseph had been traveling to Bethlehem

to be registered in the population census that the governor of the area had ordered.

They had traveled many miles.

The journey was long and slow.

Mary was seated on a donkey and Joseph walked the whole way beside her.

By the time they arrived in Bethlehem, they were tired and in need of somewhere to stay.

Joseph and Mary tried many places, but all the living space was already taken by the many visitors

who had come to Bethlehem for the census.

The town was crowded with people from all over the land.

Eventually Mary and Joseph were shown a clear, dry area where they could bed down for the night and rest.

It was a place where the animals were sheltered during winter, but which was free at this time because the weather was mild and the animals were out in the fields.

While Mary and Joseph were there, the time came for Jesus to be born.

And so it happened…and Mary and Joseph were so happy when they looked at the little child.

They could hear the angels in heaven singing with joy.

The angels were praising God and announcing the birth of this very special child.

Mary held Jesus close to her, wrapped him carefully in a blanket, and placed him in the animals' feed box, which had been carefully prepared with clean hay to make it comfortable for the tiny child.

Very soon the shepherds arrived to visit and pay homage.

They knew that Jesus was no ordinary baby and so they came from the surrounding hills to see him and to adore him.

They looked at Jesus in the animals' feed box and wondered who he really was and what his birth meant for them.

Later on, the wise men arrived.

They came from the East, riding on camels.

They brought with them special gifts of gold, incense, and perfume.

They too knew that Jesus was a special baby, so they came to worship him and bring him gifts suitable for a king.

Pray

Imagine for a moment that you are also there in Bethlehem…

that you too have come to visit.

Picture Mary and Joseph…

the shepherds…

and the wise men…

all interested in and admiring the newborn baby…

the baby who was to be the Savior of the world.

As you watch, you see Mary beckoning you to come closer.

She lifts Jesus out of the feed box and holds him in her arms so you can see him.

What does he look like?

Is he sleeping or is he awake and looking at you?

Take a moment to gaze at Jesus and remember that he is the Son of God.

You may like to say something to Jesus…

Pause

Now imagine that you have brought a gift for Jesus…

a flower…a cuddly toy…something special for him to wear.

Give your gift to Joseph.

See Joseph smile at you and hear him say thank you.

Now see yourself move back away from the baby Jesus.

Once more the shepherds and the wise men crowd around the crib.

You can see that they are excited.

You watch as they take turns to bow low and pay homage to the baby who is indeed the new born king…

the baby who is the Son of God.

Conclusion

Slowly you leave the stable and return to the classroom.

When you are ready, open your eyes and breathe deeply…in and out…in and out…in and out.

Look again at the crib and the baby photos on the prayer table/mat.

Remember that Jesus was born a baby just like you were.

He was a special baby who would grow up to become famous, because he was no ordinary baby…but truly the Son of God.

Solid as a Rock

Preparation

•Discuss with the children the presence of rocks in nature, in buildings, and other solid structures.

•Share stories that involve rocks or large stones: rock climbing, mountaineering, great walls, tombs, castles, caves, and forts.

•Identify and view pictures, videos, or slides of famous rock formations:

—the Grand Canyon;

—Mount Rushmore;

—Stonehenge;

—the pyramids.

•Discuss some of the properties of rock. Focus on its strength, reliability, endurance, and beauty.

•Encourage the children to choose and keep a pet rock which they then bring to the prayer time. Invite them to decorate their pet rocks with a personal word, symbol, or pattern.

•Gather the children around a prayer table/mat on which is placed a large rock, some smaller rocks, pictures of rock formations, a Bible, a lighted candle, and an image of Jesus.

Meditation

Read the following guided meditation to the children.

Relaxation Exercise

Place your pet rock on the floor in front of you.

Sit tall and straight, alert but relaxed.

Close your eyes and imagine you are out in the countryside sitting beside a brook or a river.

Watch the water bubble over the rocks in the river bed.

Listen to the rushing sound it makes on its way.

The sun is shining and you can hear birds chirping in the bushes nearby.

As you gaze at the water and are mesmerized by the gentle, repeating sounds of nature…

you feel warm and relaxed.

Breathe deeply and slowly and inhale the clean, fresh air of the countryside.

Breathe in and out…in and out…in and out.

Focus

Now open your eyes and pick up your pet rock.

Feel it and explore it with your hands.

Is your rock cold to touch?

Is its surface rough or smooth?

What colors can you see in your rock?

What is its shape?

Is it heavy to hold…or light?

Where did it come from?

Ponder

Now once again place your pet rock on the floor and close your eyes.

Think of places where you might find rocks…

in the garden at home…

along the roadside…

at the beach…

in the countryside…

in river beds…

under the sea…

on top of mountains.

Think how rocks are strong, solid, and reliable…

how they provide a firm base upon which to build a house.

Rocks are so strong they can withstand lightning,

rain, wind, storms, floods, and fire.

Remember how in times past rocks were used to build castles and forts with large walls surrounding them to protect people from attack by armies and enemies.

If you look closely at the surface of rocks in nature you can sometimes see tiny creatures or wildflowers and grasses living in their dents and cracks.

Rocks may also contain diamonds, precious jewels, and metals.

Rocks lying in a river bed make a beautiful picture as the water bubbles and gurgles over them, and they glint in the sunshine.

Whatever their form or shape, rocks remind us of strength and reliability.

Pray

Now let us take a few moments to pray and think about rock as an image of God.

In the Bible, God is often likened to a rock.

Like a rock, God is strong, constant, and reliable…

someone you can depend on…

someone you can trust…

someone who is always there for you…

someone who will protect you from harm.

When King David wrote his songs to God, songs which we call psalms, he wrote words like these:

I love you God, my strength.

You are my rock and my fortress,

my helper and my savior.

I take refuge in you God

because you are my rock and my shield,

my saving strength, my stronghold

and my place of refuge.

—Psalm 18:1–2 (adapted)

God can be like a rock for you too, just as he was for King David.

Like a rock, God is strong and reliable.

Like a rock, God is dependable…

God is always there for you,

loving you and caring for you.

God is with you right now and at every moment of your life.

You can always rely on God's help.

Take a few moments to talk with God…

to say that you are glad that God is always there for you.

Ask God to protect you and keep you from harm.

Pause

God wants you to know that you are precious *(Isaiah 43:4)*,

more precious than precious stones…

or the rocks in the river bed…

more precious than the birds in the air…

more precious than the flowers in the fields *(Luke 12:22–30)*.

Say thank you and whisper a prayer of love to God.

Conclusion

When you are ready, open your eyes.

Pick up your pet rock and hold it in your hands.

Look at it carefully.

Remember that your pet rock and all rocks are a reminder of God's protective love…

a reminder of God's presence in your life and in the world.

Be glad that, like King David, God is your rock, your strength, and your helper, too.

Invite children to pray together these words:

> *I love you God, my strength.*
> *You are my rock and my fortress,*
> *my helper and my savior.*
> *I take refuge in you God*
> *because you are my rock, my shield,*
> *my strength, my stronghold, and*
> *my place of protection.*
> *I love you, I praise you, and I thank you.*
>
> *—Psalm 18:1–2 (adapted)*

Encourage them to keep their pet rock as a paperweight or in a special place at home to remind them of God's presence and strong, protective love.

God's Rainbow

Preparation

•Have the children wear or bring something that represents a favorite color.

•Prepare a representation of a rainbow and place it on a prayer mat/table:

— class rainbow collage;

— lengths of ribbon or material arranged to form a rainbow;

— a large picture of a rainbow.

•Place a Bible on the prayer mat/table and open it at the story of Noah and the rainbow *(Genesis 9:8–17)*.

•Invite the children to gather around the rainbow symbol.

•Make sure you are familiar with and able to relate the story of God's rainbow from the book of Genesis.

Meditation

Read the following guided meditation to the children.

Relaxation Exercise

Today we are going to talk with God about the rainbow we sometimes see in the sky.

Sit tall and straight with your legs crossed.

Let your hands rest loosely in your lap.

Close your eyes.

Breathe deeply and quietly…in and out…in and out.

Let your body feel calm, relaxed, and very, very quiet.

Focus

Open your eyes and look at the color you are wearing

or have brought with you to our prayer time.

Think why this color is special for you.

Invite some children to show and name their favorite color, ensuring that there is a variety of colors represented.

Ponder

Now look carefully at the rainbow on our prayer mat/table.

Notice the colors that make up the rainbow.

All of our favorite colors can be found in the colors of the rainbow.

Colors are God's special gift to us.

Tell the children the story of God's rainbow (Genesis 9:8–17).

When we see a rainbow in the sky, we remember God is watching over us and caring for us.

Pray

Close your eyes and picture a rainbow in the sky.

Imagine you are traveling across the rainbow from one end to the other.

See yourself climbing up one side and sliding down the other.

At the end of the rainbow you find a beautiful garden filled with your favorite color and all the colors of the rainbow.

God is in this beautiful garden too, enjoying the colors and the perfume of the flowers.

Go over to God and say hello.

Listen to God ask you if you like the colorful rainbow.

Hear God tell you how the rainbow was made to remind you that God is always close to you, loving you, helping you, and protecting you.

Let God take you by the hand.

Spend some time together just looking at God's magnificent rainbow.

See its colors streaking across the sky…

red…yellow…purple…green…orange…blue.

As you gaze at the rainbow, remember that it is a sign of God's love for you.

Thank God for giving you this sign and the beautiful colors of the rainbow.

Pause

Now say good-bye to God and travel back across the rainbow.

As you slide down to its beginning, feel yourself land firmly on the earth.

Take a moment to look back at the rainbow in the sky…and remember that it is a sign of God's special promise to be near you always.

Conclusion

When you are ready open your eyes and return to the classroom.

Breathe in and out…in and out.

Look again at our class rainbow and at the favorite color you are wearing.

Remember that these colors are part of God's rainbow...God's promise to you of love and protection.

Invite children to write a poem about the rainbow or to rewrite Noah's story.

Bread of Life

Preparation

•Discuss with the children the importance of bread as food for our bodies.

•Discuss and/or demonstrate how bread is made. Make a distinction between leavened and unleavened bread.

•Share with the children the story of how communion hosts are made so that they understand they are a form of unleavened bread.

•Prepare a prayer table/mat on which are placed:

    —some wheat sheaves;

    —a loaf of ordinary bread;

    —some unleavened bread (pita bread);

    —a picture of Jesus at the Last Supper; and

    —some unconsecrated communion breads.

•Gather the children around the prayer mat/table.

Meditation

Read the following guided meditation to the children.

Relaxation Exercise

Today we are going to talk with Jesus about the special bread of Holy Communion.

Close your eyes and imagine you are in the country.

In front of you is a large field of wheat.

As you watch you are amazed at the golden color of the wheat and how graceful it looks swaying in the gentle breeze.

Imagine yourself swaying along with the wheat.

Breathe in the clean fresh country air.

Breathe in and out…in and out…in and out.

Watch the wheat as it moves back and forth…and let your body feel relaxed and at peace.

Focus

Open your eyes and look at the sheaves of wheat and the different breads on the prayer mat.

Remember that all of these breads are made from wheat or other grains which grow in the fields.

Recall the way wheat becomes bread…

how it is harvested, crushed into flour…

mixed with water, kneaded, and baked.

Remember that many people are involved in producing the bread we eat and the special bread, the hosts, that become Holy Communion for us at Mass.

Now look again at the breads on the mat.

The loaf of bread and pita bread provide food for our bodies.

They help us to grow up healthy and strong.

The communion hosts are also made from wheat.

When these are consecrated at Mass, they bring Jesus into our lives as the Bread of Life, bread for our souls.

Ponder

Let us think for a few moments about this special bread…

about Jesus' life and his promise to be one with us in the breaking and sharing of bread at Eucharist.

When Jesus was on the earth, just before he died, he had a special meal with his friends.

During this meal, Jesus took some bread, gave thanks to God, broke it, and gave it to his friends, saying:

This is my Body which is given for you.
Do this in memory of me (Luke 22:19).

Throughout hundreds of years, Christians have come together to bless, break, and share this special bread…

bread which in the Eucharist becomes Jesus' Bread of Life for us.

When we receive Holy Communion, we become one with Jesus.

In the same way that ordinary bread becomes part of our human bodies making us healthy and strong, Jesus comes to us in Holy Communion to nourish and strengthen us on our faith journey…our spiritual journey with God.

Holy Communion makes us healthy and strong Christians…people who are better able to bring the love of God to our families, our friends, and our world.

Jesus' gift of himself to us in Holy Communion is a wonderful and powerful mystery.

It is something that we cannot explain, but which we believe because Jesus is the Son of God and his word is true.

In Holy Communion, Jesus comes to each one of us.

Sharing this mystery together makes us one with each other in Jesus.

We are joined together in a special way with Jesus in the family of God.

Pray

Close your eyes now and imagine you are entering into a place deep inside yourself...perhaps your heart where Jesus is always present and waiting for you.

See yourself move slowly toward Jesus and sit down beside him.

Listen as Jesus tells you that the bread of Holy Communion is truly himself...

that he comes to you to be with you as your friend and helper...

to bring you all the gifts and strength you need to live a good Christian life...

a life of loving and caring for yourself, your friends, and your family.

Listen as Jesus explains to you that you and he become one through this wonderful sacrament.

Think about this for a moment!

Jesus becomes one with you...

Jesus comes to you as food...

He is the Bread of Life.

Pause

Think how Jesus can truly change your heart to make it like his...kind, honest, strong, generous, and prayerful.

Ask Jesus to do this for you...to help you become more like him in your actions and words.

Thank Jesus for all the goodness that is in you and for your faith.

Ask Jesus to help you believe always in the mystery of his presence in Holy Communion.

Tell Jesus you would like to receive Holy Communion often.

See Jesus place his hands on your head and bless you.

Hear him tell you how sharing his life with you and being your friend makes him happy.

Conclusion

Now say good-bye to Jesus and slowly return to the classroom.

Open your eyes and look at the wheat sheaves.

Remember how they grow in the fields and sway in the breeze…in the fresh country air.

Take a few slow deep breaths…in and out…in and out…in and out.

Look again at the breads on the table and remember how they provide food for your body and, when consecrated, food for your soul.

Remember, when you receive Holy Communion at Mass, Jesus is truly there for you.

Jesus comes to you to be one with you and to help you grow into a strong and loving person in the family of God.

Two Pieces of Wood

This meditation is best prayed during Holy Week.

Preparation

•Have the children make simple, individual crosses from palm leaves, ice-cream sticks or twigs bound together with wool.

•Prepare a prayer table or mat. Cover it with a purple cloth. Place on the table/mat a large crucifix, some rocks, a large purple candle and, if available, a few sprigs of thornbush.

•Invite the children to bring their crosses and gather around the prayer table/mat.

Meditation

Read the following guided meditation to the children.

Relaxation Exercise

Today we are going to talk with Jesus about the meaning of the cross.

Sit tall and straight with your legs crossed.

Place your cross on the floor in front of you.

Rest your hands loosely in your lap.

Close your eyes and tell your body to relax.

Breathe deeply and slowly in and out…in and out…in and out.

Let all the stiffness go out of you.

Move your head slowly around in a circle.

Lift your shoulders up and down.

Feel comfortable and relaxed.

Focus

Open your eyes and pick up your handmade cross.

When you see a cross, what do you think of?

Allow the children time to respond. Remind them of the importance of the cross to Christians: Jesus died on a cross because he loves us and because he wanted to save us from our sins.

The cross reminds us of Jesus' great love for each one of us.

Jesus' death on the cross enables us to share one day in the peace and joy of heaven.

Ponder

Place your cross on the floor in front of you.

Now look carefully at the crucifix on the prayer table/mat.

The soldiers treated Jesus very badly.

They spat on him and laughed at him…

they made a crown of thorns and put it on his head…

they nailed him to a cross…

and they pierced his side with a spear.

When Jesus died on the cross, he endured great suffering.

When we see a crucifix, we remember how Jesus suffered on the cross, how he suffered because he wanted to save us from sin and make it possible for us to enter heaven.

Pray

Now close your eyes and in your imagination go into your heart or special place where Jesus is waiting alive and well.

Picture Jesus sitting beside you as your friend.

See him dressed in a long white garment.

Listen to Jesus as he tells you that he loves you.

He wants you to be happy here on earth and one day to be with him in heaven.

But the way to heaven is not always easy.

Hear Jesus tell you that the journey of life can sometimes be very difficult.

Everyone experiences disappointments, suffering, and hurt at some time in their lives.

Hear Jesus tell you that even though suffering is a part of life, such times are not forever…they do pass.

Good feelings and good times will follow bad times.

Listen to Jesus tell you that you can grow and become strong during these difficult times…if you do not let them get you down.

Jesus reminds you how he is always close to you to help you through the trials and disappointments of life.

Tell Jesus how you feel when someone disappoints you or something sad or hurtful happens to you.

Ask him to help you be strong when troubles come.

Hear Jesus tell you again that he is always beside you, in good times and in bad.

He knows what it is like to feel sadness, suffering and hurt…and he is always there to comfort you and to be your friend.

Tell Jesus you are glad he is your friend.

Remember that you can talk to him at any time about all the things that worry or hurt you.

Conclusion

Watch Jesus now as he stands up and prepares to leave.

You might like to shake hands with him and tell him you will talk again with him sometime soon.

Leave Jesus and return to the classroom.

Concentrate again on your breathing.

Breathe in and out slowly and quietly.

Move your shoulders up and down.

Move your head slowly around in a circle.

When you are ready, open your eyes.

Pick up your handmade cross.

Look at it for a moment.

Remember that it is a sign of Jesus' love for you and a promise of help in times of trouble.

Now look again at the crucifix on the prayer table/mat.

Remember that Jesus suffered and died for us to free us from sin and make it possible for us to go to heaven.

Thank Jesus for dying on the cross for us.

Say together the following prayer:

> *We adore you Jesus and we praise you*
> *because by your cross you have saved the world.*

At another time lead the children through the Stations of the Cross.

Easter Eggs and the Empty Tomb

This meditation is best prayed immediately after Easter.

Preparation

Gather the children around a prayer mat on which is placed:

• one large hollow chocolate Easter egg wrapped in brightly colored paper;

• an unlit candle;

• a Bible opened at a picture of the risen Jesus;

• a hand-crafted representation (or picture) of the empty tomb on the morning of the resurrection.

Meditation

Read the following guided meditation to the children.

Relaxation Exercise

Today, the focus of our meditation is the wonderful event of Jesus' resurrection, which is celebrated at Easter time.

Sit tall but comfortably on the floor with your legs crossed.

Rest your hands loosely in your lap.

Close your eyes and breathe deeply.

This helps your body to relax.

Breathe in and out and concentrate on your breathing.

Feel the air coming into your body…in through your nose…

and down into your lungs… filling you with freshness and life.

Breathe in and out…in and out…in and out.

Feel comfortable and relaxed.

Focus

Now open your eyes and look at the large Easter egg on the prayer mat.

Notice also the empty tomb, the unlit candle, and the picture of Jesus risen from the dead.

All of these are connected with our celebration of Easter.

In our prayer today, we are going to think about these connections…and what this great feast means for us.

Pick up the Easter egg and hold it up for all to see.

Let us focus our attention first on the Easter egg.

Look at the brightly colored wrapping paper which is a sign of joy and celebration.

Unwrap the egg.

As I unwrap the paper you can see the chocolate egg emerging.

The egg reminds us of the beginning of life…of new life…like the chicken that is hatched out of a real egg in the farm yard or incubator.

Place the egg on the floor and break it.

When we break the chocolate egg open, we can see that inside the egg there is nothing.

The egg is empty—like the empty tomb from which Jesus rose at Easter time.

Place the broken Easter egg back on the prayer mat next to the unlit candle.

Before we share our Easter egg, let us take a few moments more to think about its meaning for us as Christians.

Ponder

Close your eyes and imagine you are in a beautiful garden.

At the end of the garden there is a large tomb carved out of the side of the rock face.

Imagine that this is the tomb where Jesus was laid after he died on the cross…

It is a large hole in the side of a hill…closed over by a heavy boulder that fitted across the opening like a door.

As you come closer, you can see that the boulder is rolled back.

You look inside the tomb and see that it is empty.

You wonder what this means.

You ask yourself, "Where is Jesus' body?"

Then, just as you are about to leave, you hear a voice calling you.

You turn around and see Jesus standing close by.

He is calling you to come and join him.

You notice how great he looks.

His clothes are bright and shiny.

He is excited, happy, and smiling at you…

wanting you to know that he is alive…

that he is risen from the dead and wants to share his excitement with you.

Pray

See yourself walk over to Jesus.

You are happy to see him.

Listen as he tells you that God raised him from the dead...

that the tomb is no longer his resting place...

that he has overcome death to rise to a new life...

a life that will never end...

a life that he will spend with his God in heaven.

Listen as Jesus tells you that he will never die again...

that he will always be alive...

and always be there for you.

Tell Jesus that you are glad he is alive.

Ask him to help you believe in him always...

to follow his ways of bringing peace and love, healing and joy to everyone in our world.

Listen as Jesus tells you he loves you.

Say thank you to Jesus.

Pause

It is time now to leave Jesus near the empty tomb in the beautiful garden.

In your imagination, see yourself begin to walk away from the rocky tomb.

As you do so, you turn around to take one last look at Jesus and to wave good-bye.

But Jesus is no longer there!

All you can see is the open tomb...a large dark hole carved out of the rock.

You continue to walk slowly away from the tomb and out of the garden.

In your heart you know that Jesus will always be close, even though you cannot see him.

You smile to yourself and feel happy.

Conclusion

Make your way back along the path and return to the classroom.

Focus again on your breathing.

Breathe deeply and slowly in and out…in and out.

When you are ready, open your eyes and look again at the symbols of Easter on the prayer mat.

Light the candle.

As we light our Easter candle, we remember it is a sign that Jesus is alive and is with us.

The candle, the empty tomb, and the Easter egg all remind us of the presence of Jesus.

Whenever we light a candle for prayer, we remember the presence of Jesus among us.

Share the Easter egg with the children.

Holy Spirit: Hero within Me

Preparation

• Name and share stories of modern day heroes/heroines such as:

— peace workers (missionaries, Peace Corps)

— humanitarian workers (Dorothy Day, Peter Maurin)

— saints (Mother Teresa, Pope John XXIII)

— community volunteers (firefighters, St. Vincent de Paul Society, Salvation Army)

• Discuss with the children the concept of hero/heroine. Identify attributes and values that lead people to perform heroic deeds:

— respect for human life

— relationship with God

— love for all people

— desire to serve, help, heal others

— dedication to a cause

• Reflect on the life of Jesus, who is the ultimate hero and model for all Christian heroes and heroines. Share with the children examples from Jesus' life that made him a hero with the people of his time…and all time.

• Have the children prepare personal profiles of heroic people highlighting the Christian (Christlike) attributes and values that motivate and sustain them in their lives.

• Gather the class for prayer around a prayer table/mat. Make sure that each child has his/her profile of a chosen hero/heroine before them. On the prayer table/mat have a picture of Jesus, a Bible, and a lighted candle (symbol of the presence of Jesus and his Spirit among us).

Meditation

Read the following guided meditation to the children.

Relaxation Exercise

Today we are going to pray about heroes and heroines and especially about the Spirit of Jesus who is God's gift to each one of us.

Sit straight and tall, alert but relaxed.

Move your shoulders up and down a few times and shake all the tension out of your body.

Breathe deeply and slowly…in and out…in and out.

Feel the life-giving air moving in and out of your body.

Continue to breathe this way a few times until you feel relaxed and contented.

Focus

Look at the profile of your chosen hero/heroine.

Recall the actions that make this person special.

Choose one activity or characteristic that makes the person you have chosen a real hero or heroine.

Invite some children to share with the class the particular heroic activity or characteristic they have chosen.

Real heroes/heroines are people who do ordinary things extraordinarily well.

Real heroes/heroines go out of their way to help others.

They are people who seem to have something extra…extra love…extra generosity…extra strength in times of trouble…extra compassion…and a great capacity for helping others.

They care about other people and our world.

Ponder

Close your eyes now and take a few moments to think about where these extra qualities come from.

Jesus tells us that they come from the Spirit of God who lives within us.

The Holy Spirit is given to us at baptism and helps us to be like Jesus…the Spirit teaches us…encourages us…and strengthens us in our Christian lives.

The same Spirit was in Jesus…and urged Jesus

To bring good news to the poor;

to soothe the broken-hearted;

to give sight to the blind and

to set people free.

(From Luke 4:18)

Throughout the centuries many people have been inspired by Jesus to follow in his footsteps.

Many people have been led by the Holy Spirit to become like Jesus…to become heroes and heroines in their time.

We too can call on the Holy Spirit to help us to be like these heroes and heroines…

to be like Jesus…because the Spirit of Jesus lives within us too.

Pray

Keep your eyes closed and go into your heart or special place where you can talk with Jesus.

See him waiting for you.

Imagine yourself sitting beside Jesus and listening to him tell you about the wonderful gift of the Holy Spirit that you have been given.

Jesus tells you how it was by the power of the Holy Spirit that he was able to do so many good things…

how it was the Spirit of God that filled him with love and strength and compassion.

Listen as Jesus tells you that you too have this special gift of the Holy Spirit and that the Holy Spirit will help you to pray…

to know what is right and wrong…

to be strong and good…

to be kind and helpful to others.

Ask Jesus to open your heart and mind to the gift of his Spirit so that you can be more like him…

and more like all the wonderful people who have followed his ways to become heroes and heroines of goodness.

Pause

When you have finished talking with Jesus, you and he stand up together and you prepare to leave your heart or special place.

As you do, imagine that Jesus blesses you with a sign of the cross on your forehead.

This is a reminder of his special gift to you…

the gift of his Spirit who will stay with you and help you.

Say thank you to Jesus.

Conclusion

Now leave your heart or special place and return to the classroom.

Breathe slowly and deliberately…in and out…in and out…in and out.

Remember that the Holy Spirit is with you always…

the Spirit of goodness, peace and love…

the Spirit of all true heroes and heroines.

When you are ready, open your eyes.

Look again at the profile of your hero or heroine.

Know that you too can be like them, a hero or heroine in your own way.

You have the Holy Spirit with you to help you.

Earth Care

Preparation

•Ensure the children have been engaged in class discussion about the creatures that live in the wild and about the need to care for our earth by planting plants and trees.

•Place some seeds in small envelopes. Attach each envelope to a piece of string tied to a balloon ready for release at the end of the prayer time.

•Where possible take this prayer session outside to an area where there are healthy green plants and trees.

•Have the balloons nearby but not visible during the meditation time.

•Prepare a seed box and seeds ready for the children to plant at the conclusion of the prayer.

•If the prayer session has to be conducted inside, create a nature focus by having one or two large potted plants and some appropriate forest pictures as the centerpiece of the prayer mat/table around which you gather the children.

Meditation

Read the following guided meditation to the children.

Relaxation Exercise

Today during our prayer time, we will think and pray about how we can care for our planet earth which is God's wonderful gift to us.

Let us begin by focusing our attention on our topic by clearing our minds and relaxing our bodies so that we can better concentrate on our prayer.

Sit tall with your legs crossed and your hands resting loosely in your lap.

Take a few deep breaths and, as you do, tighten the muscles in your upper body and shoulders.

Hold for a few seconds and then let go and relax.

Breathe in…hold…let go.

Breathe in…hold…and let go.

Shake your shoulders and arms a little and shake away all the tension and tightness in your body.

Focus

Look now at the trees and plants (or pictures) around you.

Notice the different shapes.

Some are tall and thin…others are shorter and thicker.

Notice the greens.

They are not all exactly the same.

Look again at the trees and plants.

Notice the color of their leaves.

Do the trees look and smell fresh and clean…or are they in need of a shower of rain to wash away the dirt and dust?

Do any of the plants or trees have flowers on them?

Are there any nuts, berries or fruit?

What colors can you see?

These plants and trees provide shade from the sun…

protection from the wind…

and a home for many of God's little creatures…

like birds…ants…ladybugs…and spiders.

Ponder

Close your eyes

and keep the picture of these beautiful trees and plants in your mind.

Imagine you are playing a game among them...

hiding from your friends or using a shrub to crawl into like a little house.

Picture some of the small creatures you find in your house...

perhaps a bird's nest...or a spider's web...or a tiny caterpillar's cocoon.

Think how precious these little creatures are...

how they are an important part of God's world and ours.

Remember that plants, trees, deserts, and forests provide a home for all creatures great and small.

Pray

Imagine you have found a special bush that you can crawl under...

a woodland house where you can be alone...

where you can talk with Jesus.

Your special place is dry and warm.

You feel very comfortable sitting under the branches.

Jesus loves this place too.

It is part of the beautiful world that God provides for all creatures.

Listen as Jesus tells you about the little creatures that have a home in the forest...

the baby birds that are born there...

the beautiful web that the spider spins in the sun to catch its prey...

the ants that feed off the sap of the branches.

Jesus cares about these tiny creatures and knows that you can too.

Thank Jesus for all the wonderful creatures of the earth—great and small.

Pause

Listen as Jesus tells you how important it is to keep growing new trees…

to cover the earth and provide a home for all God's creatures.

Tell Jesus how you will help by caring for God's creation…

by planting seeds and getting others to do the same.

See Jesus smile with joy and bless you.

Thank him for the trees and plants and for being there with you in God's wonderful creation.

Conclusion

Now leave your woodland house.

When you are ready, open your eyes and join your classmates and friends again in the playground (or classroom).

Breathe deeply…in and out…in and out…in and out.

Remember your promise to Jesus to help grow more trees and plants for the earth.

We are now going to release our balloons and plant our seeds.

The balloons and envelopes of seeds carry a message for others to join us in our activity.

Invite the children to release the balloons into the atmosphere. Then, have them plant their own seeds in the carefully prepared seed box.

The Summer Sun

Preparation

• Have the children participate in classroom discussion about their experiences of summertime.

• Prepare pictures and symbols of summer. These could be:

— a large collage prepared by the class;

— individual pictures drawn by each child;

— a collection of summer symbols such as a beach ball, flowers, sand, sunglasses.

• Arrange the pictures and symbols on a prayer mat along with a lighted candle, your class Bible, and a picture of Jesus.

• Gather the children around the prayer mat.

Meditation

Read the following guided meditation to the children.

Relaxation Exercise

Today we are going to talk with God about summertime and the summer sun.

First we will prepare for our prayer by making sure we are relaxed.

Close your eyes and take a deep breath into your body.

Slowly and quietly let the breath out again into the room.

Do this calmly a few times.

Feel the air going in through your nose and down into your lungs, filling them with freshness and life.

Breathe in...out...in...out...in...out.

Let the air help you to feel comfortable and relaxed.

Focus

Open your eyes and look at the pictures and symbols of summertime.

Summertime is vacation time.

In your mind think about your favorite picture or symbol.

What does it remind you of...

running barefoot around the house...

walking in the shade...

a day at the beach...

playing in the pool...

watering the garden?

Think of some words to describe how you feel during summertime...

hot

tired

sweaty

sleepy

warm

cool by the sea

happy

carefree

relaxed

Ponder

Close your eyes and think about the summer sun.

See it high in the sky like a large golden ball...

warming the earth and making all things bright and colorful.

Feel its rays surrounding you.

Feel its warmth on your face.

See yourself cover your eyes to protect them from the glare.

The sun's rays are strong and powerful.

They can burn our skin, making us red and sore.

The sun is one of God's wonderful creations but it must be respected.

The sun makes things grow and it makes them wither.

It gives us warmth but it can also burn.

The sun is beautiful.

In the daytime it makes all things shiny and bright.

In the evening it changes the color of the sky, making it red and orange, pink and white.

The sun is one of God's special gifts to our world.

We are happy when the sun is shining.

Pray

Keeping your eyes closed, take a moment now to talk with God about the sun and summertime.

Tell God what you like about the sun.

Pause

Listen to God say thank you. God likes to hear you praise creation.

Listen as God tells you to be careful in the sun…

to enjoy its warmth but to respect its power.

Tell God what you like about summertime.

Share with God some of the things you like to do.

See God listening to you and enjoying your story.

Pause

Thank God again for the wonderful gift of the sun.

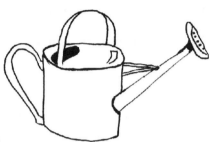

Conclusion

Now it is time for you to return to the classroom.

Concentrate again on your breathing.

Breathe slowly and deeply…in…out…in…out…in…out…in…out.

When you are ready, open your eyes.

Look again at the pictures and symbols on the prayer mat.

Remember always to be grateful to God for the sun and summertime.

Together we will sing (or say) a short psalm of praise for God's beautiful creation.

> *Praise God, praise God.*
> *O God, how great you are,*
> *clothed in majesty and glory,*
> *wearing light as your cloak.*
>
> *You made the moon to mark out the seasons.*
> *The sun knows when to set.*
> *You have made all things well, O God.*
> *The earth is filled with your greatness.*
> *Praise God, praise God.*
> *O God, how great you are!*
>
> *—Psalm 104:1–2, 19, 24 (adapted)*

Of Related Interest. . .

Prayer Services for Young Children

30 Ten-Minute Celebrations
GAYLE SCHREIBER

Thirty 10-minute prayer services center on themes easily understood by preschool and primary grade children. Each service includes: an original song, greeting, short verse from Scripture, group response, symbol, and "Thank You" prayer.

ISBN: 0-89622-542-9, 72 pp, $9.95

Stories, Symbols, Songs and Skits for Lively Children's Liturgies

ANNE MARIE LEE
AND ELAINE WISDOM

A spirited handbook of suggestions for parish leaders and liturgists to involve children and gain fuller participation in liturgy preparation. Offers a cornucopia of student-involving techniques.

ISBN: 089622-640-9, 88 pp, $9.95

On Audiobook

Leading Children to God

GWEN COSTELLO

This four-part audio program focuses on ways that catechists and teachers can help children build a relationship with God. Listeners are challenged to examine their own habits of communicating with God.

Two 35-min cassettes, $16.95 (A-76)

Ways to Pray with Children

Prayers, Activities, and Services
BARBARA ANN BRETHERTON

This resource for teachers, catechists, and parents teaches how to make prayer practical, enjoyable, easily accessible, and relevant in the lives of children. Offers suggestions on incorporating prayer into children's lives and describes many different forms of prayer.

ISBN: 089622-670-0, 80 pp, $9.95

Learning by Doing

150 Activities to Enrich Religion Classes for Young Children
CAROLE MACCLENNAN

A systematic yet simple "lesson wheel" approach where the lesson is seen as a wheel with a hub (topic) that is connected by spokes (sensory activities designed to engage the attention of young children) to the rim (completed objectives).

ISBN: 0-89622-562-3, 136 pp, $14.95

Available at religious bookstores or from:

XXIII TWENTY-THIRD PUBLICATIONS
P.O. Box 180 • Mystic, CT 06355

1-800-321-0411 • E-Mail:ttpubs@aol.com